HAVE YOU EVER WONDERED HOW BOOKS ARE MADE?

Fox & Ink Books (formerly UCLan Publishing) is an award-winning independent publisher. Based at the University of Lancashire, this Preston-based publisher teaches MA Publishing students how to become industry professionals using the content and resources from its business; students are included at every stage of the publishing process and credited for the work that they contribute.

The business doesn't just help publishing students though. Fox & Ink Books has supported the employability and real-life work skills for the University's Illustration, Acting, Translation, Animation, Photography, Film & TV students and many more. This is the beauty of books and stories; they fuel many other creative industries! The MA Publishing students are able to get involved from day one with the business and they acquire a behind-the-scenes experience of what it is like to work for a such a reputable independent.

The MA course was awarded a Times Higher Award (2018) for Innovation in the Arts, and the business was awarded Best Newcomer at the Independent Publishing Guild (2019) for the ethos of teaching publishing using a commercial publishing house. As the business continues to grow, so too does the student experience upon entering this dynamic Master's course.

www.foxandinkbooks.com
www.foxandinkbooks.com/courses/
foxandink@lancashire.ac.uk

This book is dedicated to every mum who has ever shed a tear (or two) reading one of my poems.

And to my own mum, who is simply my very best friend.

All of My Days is a Fox & Ink Books book

First published in Great Britain in 2026 by
Fox & Ink Books
part of the University of Lancashire
Preston, PR1 2HE, UK

Text and illustrations copyright © Kerri Cunningham, 2026

978-1-917894-01-2

1 3 5 7 9 10 8 6 4 2

The right of Kerri Cunningham to be identified as the author
and illustrator of this work has been asserted in accordance
with the Copyright, Designs and Patents Act, 1988.

All rights reserved. No part of this publication may be reproduced,
stored in a retrieval system, or transmitted in any form or by any means,
electronic, mechanical, photocopying, recording or otherwise;
or be used to train any AI technologies without the prior permission
of the publishers. Fox & Ink Books expressly reserves this work from
the text and data mining exception subject to EU law.

Set in Kingfisher by Becky Chilcott.

A CIP catalogue record for this book is available from the British Library.

Printed and bound in Great Britain by Page Bros Ltd., Mile Cross Lane, Norwich, NR6 6SA.

Murphy's Sketches

All of my days

Fox & Ink Books

Foreword

I've always been an emotional person. Sometimes I feel like I've spent my whole life on the brink of tears or on the brink of hysterical laughter, without much in between. Everything has always felt . . . a lot to me. That's the only way I can describe it. So when I became a mum, and I was faced with all the emotions that come along with that, it knocked me off my feet.

I always wanted to be a mum – it just wasn't exactly next on my to-do list when it happened. I finally had a grown-up job that I liked well enough, I lived with my best friend in our cosy little girl flat. Everything was just slotting into place, and then life threw me a curveball in the shape of a true angel: my eldest son.

I didn't really do the whole preparing-for-a-newborn thing very well. I sort of imagined everything would go back to how it was before: I'd be sat back at my desk in no time, my body would magically transform over night from pregnant to totally back to normal, my social life would start back up again immediately whilst someone looked after my little bundle of joy. I just didn't ever sit down and think about what was actually going to happen when he arrived. But the thing I learnt was that no one – no matter how many books they read, how many antenatal classes they attended, how many weeks they spent trying for a baby, wishing, hoping, praying – not one of them ever could predict what would happen in that moment when you hold your child for the first time.

For me, it was true euphoria. It was love at first sight, totally confirmed on the spot by this little heartbeat that was placed on my chest, all soft and warm skin that felt as natural as my own. The memories I have of labour are scattered and blurred, but I do remember so vividly his bright eyes locked mine, and my heart was forever changed. It felt like an entire lifetime had been leading to this perfect moment: he was here, and I was his mum.

I was never the same again: being a mum altered every single bit of me, and I didn't find it easy. I loved him more than anything, but all those emotions I had struggled with my whole life now felt so loud, so impossible to ignore. As much happiness as it brought me, it equally brought me fear, sadness, anxiety – could I keep this perfect person safe, happy, healthy in such an imperfect world? Was I actually any 'good' at being his mum? Did I deserve him?

I hid my worries away for a long time, and I thought that I was the only mum who felt the way I did – but of course that's never the case. Two more babies and two more hits of that love-at-first-sight euphoria later, I started sharing bits of writing on my Instagram page, opening up a little bit about my struggles with anxiety after becoming a mum, or just little poems about having a child and everyday life. Some of it was silly, and some of it was me really laying my soul bare. In hindsight, I think I was looking for some help, some reassurance . . . and I found it.

I realised that there were other mums out there – lots of them – who felt exactly the same way I did. Who had suffered postnatal anxiety, or who had intrusive thoughts, or who just simply loved their kids so blooming much that they felt totally overwhelmed by that love. With their support, I kept writing and creating and sharing my words, inspired by my own experiences with my children. I wrote not just for me but for those mothers too, who might not have had the words to say how they felt, or who might not have felt like they wanted to share them just yet.

Perhaps you are one of those mums, or perhaps you've been

gifted this book by one of them. Either way, I want to say thank you. You've helped me to find my voice and set free the words that were kept inside my head and my heart for too long.

And now here they are in the form of this book. There are poems that celebrate the very beginning of becoming a mother, poems that will reassure you that you're doing a good job, poems that will rejoice in those wonderful connections we make with each other as mothers, poems that will let you know you're not alone if you're struggling, poems that will shine a golden light on those beautiful, everyday moments of being a mum – which to me is just the most wonderful thing I have ever done.

Once, someone told me that my words and illustrations will always remind them of when their children were little, and I hope that this book can feel that way for some of you. I hope the words bring you comfort, that they make you smile as much as they might make you cry, that they validate your feelings, and that they become reminiscent of this time of your life as a mother.

I hope that you enjoy them.

love, Kerri x

Welcome to Motherhood

All Of My Days

When I first looked at your face,
And into your eyes,
I saw the reason for my entire existence.
And I knew that my purpose
Was simply to love you,
All of my days.

Welcome to Motherhood

Welcome to motherhood.
At times you're going to feel
Overwhelmed, exhausted, scared, confused,
   overworked, hungry, thirsty.
You're going to really need to wee
but you'll be trapped under someone sleeping,
when you yourself might not have slept for days.
You're going to work hard.
Maybe harder than you ever have before.
And it won't be easy.
BUT...
You are always going to feel loved.
You will always have a best friend.
(Maybe more than one.)
You are going to feel joy and happiness every single day.
Even on the hard ones.
And no matter how overwhelmed, exhausted,
   scared, confused, overworked, or tired you are,
you're going to do a great job.
Because you are a mum.
The best mum they could ever have.

My Reason

That wave of fear drew out,
To let that tide of love rush in.
I was surrounded by calm water,
When I felt our skin on skin.
I knew I'd always have an anchor now,
To pull me to the shore.
I had a reason to keep floating,
That I'd never had before.
My whole life I'd felt shipwrecked,
Now I was no longer lost at sea.
I found a calm within my storm,
I had a reason just to be.

The Plan

I had a plan.
I had a bag.
Folded all neatly,
The things that I'd need.
I'd been to classes,
Read some books.
They told me, "You'll KNOW
When to push, how to breathe."

There wasn't
Any warning –
How plans can all change
In the blink of an eye.
And when it did,
I knew nothing –
What had happened,
The how or the why.

For months
I'd try to run through it.
But the details,
They all became blurred.
The sounds,
The smells, the lights,
Their faces.
I'd never been so scared.

The guilt
Was overwhelming.
It was never my fault,
But that's just how it feels.
My baby
Got here safely,
I was lucky, I know,
But my mind didn't heal.

It took
A long time to accept
There was nothing
That I could have done.
The trauma
I went through in childbirth,
Didn't make me any less of a mum.

The Bubble

Tea and toast,
Brew and biscuits,
Milky chops and soggy tops.

One-handed dinners,
Ten-second showers,
Those little toes and tiny clothes.

Hundreds of photos,
Hundreds of nappies,
That new baby smell on their soft fluffy head.

Chaos and calm,
Joy and despair,
Midnight cuddles snuggled up on the bed.

We Are Beautiful

We are told to love our bodies
Because they created life,
Whilst also being told to 'bounce back'
In record time.
That we must quickly erase
Any evidence at all
That they were once a home to our babies.
It's okay if you struggle to love a body
you don't recognise.
Or if you don't ever 'bounce back'
(whatever that even means).
Our bodies change so much
when we become a mum.
Some of us don't recognise ourselves at all
when we look in the mirror.
And some of us don't like what we see,
And some of us feel exactly the same as before.
If you don't feel like 'you'
Mentally or physically, after having children,
I hope one day you do.
And that you feel happy and comfortable
in your own skin.
And I hope that you know
that you don't have to change yourself to feel that way.
But until then, know this:
You are NOT alone.

So many of us feel the same way,
And we're embarrassed or too sad to talk about it.
But we are beautiful,
Even if we can't see it yet.
Especially to those babies
Who still think of us as
their home.

Everything You Need to Be

When I became a mum,
I thought I had to become superhuman.
But I was so wrong.
I had to become more human than I'd ever been before.
I had to feel more deeply,
I had to love like I had never loved before.
I had to confront my worst fears,
And face every one of my flaws,
And see that in spite of all of them,
I was already everything I needed to be.

The Greatest Gift

Last year you were a wish,
This year you're here with me.
The greatest gift there ever was,
And there will ever be.

A Family

You grow up thinking,
"I'll have a family".
Like it's as simple
As having a biscuit,
Or a chippy tea.
Like it will happen overnight,
Or like magic.
"I will have a family!"
And they just appear.
You never think
You might struggle to meet
Someone to have a family with.
You never think
You might meet the perfect person
To have a family with,
And then struggle to conceive.
You never think
you'll get pregnant,
And then lose a baby.
You never think
You'll have a baby,
And then struggle with postnatal depression.
You never think
you'll have a family with someone,
And then grow apart.
We grow up thinking

That having a family
Is such an easy thing.
That it's a given –
And it isn't.
It's a struggle,
For so many of us.
But it's a struggle
That is always worth it.
Because having a family,
It *is* magic.
It is like the best biscuit
Or chippy tea you've ever had
In your whole life.
It is worth every struggle,
Every fight,
Every single heartache.
Family is worth every second of it.

little one

Little one
Who I adore,
I'm not sure
What was before.
Before there was you,
What did I do
With my hands, or my time?
I haven't a clue.
Now they're both full up,
And so is my heart.
It has been since the very start.
The day that I laid my eyes on you,
And knew my dreams
Had all come true.

There's No Map

When you feel that you're lost in it,
Just know there's no map for this role.
At times it can seem like
You've lost the path,
And there's nothing that you can control.
It's a funny old journey at times –
It can feel like it's swallowed you whole.
But you're okay,
And you will find a way,
Just give it your heart and your soul.

We Were Made For Each Other

The moment that we met,
It was love at first sight
And forever.
I thanked every single star above
That we were brought together.
By the universe or fate,
Or whatever powers that be,
I knew that I was made for you
And you were made for me.
In each other we found home
When we became a family.

Hey, Mum

Hey, Mum,
I know you're tired.
I'm kind of sleepy, too.
But as I lay there in my bed,
I started missing you.
I thought it would be nicer
To sit with you a while.
Hear you sing a song or two –
That always makes me smile.
I just find it so soothing,
To listen to your voice.
And in your arms is where I'd stay,
If I could have my choice.
I thought it would be lovely
For you to stroke my face,
Or just to lie beside you.
That's my favourite place.
Mummy, I am sorry,
I know it's time for bed.
But right here on your chest
Is where I think I'll rest my head.

I Needed You

You need me for everything,
I take care of you.
Whatever it is you need from me,
Well that's just what I'll do.

You need me for everything,
For comfort, food, to play.
Whatever it is that you need me to do,
That's how I'll fill my days.

But something caught me by surprise,
Something I never knew.
I never even realised
How much I needed you.

So you can ask for anything,
And when you call, I'll come.
Because what I'd always needed
Was to become your mum.

To Be a Mother

To be a Mother
Is simply this:
Take out your very heart and soul,
And watch them walk around the world
Without you.
If they hurt,
You hurt.
If they feel joy,
You feel joy.
You will be apart,
And yet forever connected.
You will always walk to that same beat.
Together always.

Little Feet, Little Steps

Little feet suddenly taking
Little steps across the floor.
But it doesn't seem a minute
Since we brought you through the door.

Little feet that step towards me,
Little steps with arms stretched out.
I'll pick you up each time you fall
And come whenever you shout.

Little feet, you just go steady.
Little steps, you take your time.
Those little feet will have adventures –
They'll find mountains they can climb.

Little feet that keep on trying.
Little steps, Now off you go.
I'm so proud of all those little steps,
But now I want time to slow.
It's bittersweet,
Those little feet,
Just how quickly they do grow.

No Perfect Mother

I'm a Mum

I'm a mum,
So are you.
So I won't judge
The things you do.
I might work,
You might not.
You might have things
I've not got.
You might co-sleep,
But I don't.
I might breastfeed,
But you won't.
I won't eye-roll,
Tut or frown.
What good will it do me,
To put you down?
There's no right or wrong,
This isn't a test.
We're all just trying
To do our best.

Nana

Where would I be without you?
You were Mum,
Now you're so much more.
I can't even count the times
That you've been by my side,
Picked me up off the floor.
You always have the answer –
I don't know how,
You just do.
I'll be a wonderful mother
If I can be
Even half of you.

Pizza

They bring nappies like everyone else,
but they also bring you a pizza.
Or a care package of face masks, bubble bath, chocolate.
Little tiny things that say, "I get it, I know".
They put their arms around you first, then they hold the baby.
They ask how you're feeling, then they ask again.
They sit in silence with you.
They don't outstay their welcome,
but they make sure you don't feel alone.
They don't offer a single word of advice, unless you ask.
Then they give it with sensitivity.
They listen. To anything and everything you want to say.
They tell you it's all valid.
They say they understand.
They make you feel like you're doing a good job.
And that if you need anyone for anything, they'll be there.

No Perfect Mother

At the end of each day, you're shattered,
So tired you can barely think.
There seems to be piles of stuff everywhere,
And dishes stacked up in the sink.
And you wonder, "Can I really do this?
Am I the best mum I could be?
When I look around at others,
At these 'perfect mothers',
They seem so much better than me."

At the end of each day, you're shattered,
Because you did the best you could do.
And your children, they go to bed happy,
Because they have a mum like you.

So tell yourself
"Yes! I CAN do this.
I am the best mum I could be."
Don't compare to others –
There are no perfect mothers.
You're everything you need to be.

It's Not Just a 'Down Day'

You haven't felt very much 'you' for a while –
You try to hide it with a smile.
They say that if you have a problem then share it,
That opening up can help to repair it.
But it's not always easy
When eyes are on you,
And you feel like you haven't a clue what to do.
For something that can come so easy to others,
It's not always the case for all of us mothers.
You worry and stress and you can't seem to rest,
You just hope people see that you're trying your best.
But the world's become scary,
You whole view has shifted.
And this haze of confusion
Can't seem to be lifted.
You hide it away
And you hope they don't see.
This just isn't the way
That you'd hoped it would be.

It's not just a 'down day',
And it's not 'baby blues'.
If only you knew
That this isn't just you.
You are not alone,
Not the first or the last.
Just know there is help,
And that this too shall pass.

A Mother to Your Soul

Some women come into our lives,
And they're a mother to us.
They might only be a few years older,
They might even be the same age,
But the love they give,
The care, the advice,
The listening ear,
The shoulder to cry on,
The arms to hold you up,
The dose of sharp reality they'll give you
If they think you've lost your way –
They're a mother to you.
It goes beyond a friendship,
They're a mother to your soul.
They may be there for the rest of your life,
They might be there just for a little while,
But you're so much better
For knowing them,
And for having them guide and protect you.

To the Wonderful Mums

To the mum who's rooting through her bag
For wipes that just aren't there.
To the mum who's wondering,
"What day was it, when I last washed my hair?"
To the mum who isn't sure what day
The books are due back in.
To the mum who thinks they may have put
The spellings in the bin.
To the mum who doesn't know
Where they put that birthday card.
To the mum who's always asking,
"Why is it so hard?"
To the mum who forgot sunscreen,
Or a coat, or gloves, or hat.
To the mum who's feeling tired, overwhelmed,
Or simply flat.
To the mum who's not got a clue
How she does it every day.
To the mum who's truly wonderful
In every single way.

You Are Their Perfect Family

You were two, now you're one.
And it's heavy,
The weight of it all,
On your shoulders alone.
It isn't quite how you had pictured it.
You get lost in your head,
When you scroll through your phone.
When you see those perfect families –
Or at least that's how it seems to you.
Holidays, Christmases, birthdays.
All of the things that you'd pictured you'd do
Together, as a family unit.
That wasn't the way that things turned out to be.
But you are stronger than you know.
You are their perfect family.

Sometimes

Sometimes
We just need to hear
"You are such a good mum."

I Will Understand

You don't ever need to justify anything to me.
You don't ever need to say,
"Sorry I haven't text you back".
You don't have to make excuses about your house being a mess,
Or your car or your hair,
Or anything at all.
(It's not a mess anyway.)
You don't need to hide your emotions
Behind a, "I'm tired"
Or, "We're not getting much sleep".
You can always cry with me,
If you need to.
I understand what it is to be stretched in one too
    many directions.
To be worn out,
Fed up,
Touched out.
I understand the toll it takes on your mind.
I understand what it feels like to be lonely,
And yet to need some space at the same time.
And I understand that sometimes we just
    need to be quiet for a while,
And I will be there whenever you want,
Or need to talk.

I Hold You

When the world gets heavy,
I hold you.
To feel the weight of you
In my arms
Makes everything so much lighter.

A Good Mum

You can be a good mum
And find it hard.
You can be a good mum
And find parts of it boring.
You can be a good mum
And need a night off.
You can be a good mum
And need a whole week off.
You can be a good mum
And never ever want to step foot in a soft play
For the rest of your whole life.
You can be a good mum,
And say that you're tired.
You can be a good mum
And have a really, really bad day.
You can be a good mum,
And have a really good moan.
You can be a good mum
In a million different ways.

So don't judge someone else's way
Because it doesn't match your own.
As long as their children are happy, healthy,
That's all that matters.

All of us are just trying to be a good mum.

That Friend

Having a mum friend
Who makes you feel comfortable,
Who looks out for your children and for you,
Who doesn't bat an eyelid when you're late,
or frazzled and overwhelmed,
Who just *gets* you . . .
Is wonderful.

Our
'Do you remember?'
Days

Home

To some it will seem like it's chaos:
Our house, it's so messy and loud.
But when I sit down at the end of each day,
I look around at this mess and feel proud.

The paint could do with a touch up.
Little jobs never seem to get done.
But there's plenty of time left to sort them –
We're busy right now having fun.

Our walls are filled up with laughter,
We make memories here in this space.
This is where we are all together,
And together is our favourite place.

When they move out and they're all grown up,
Maybe we'll move away from this place.
But don't worry, it isn't the house or the walls –
They'll see home when they look at your face.

So, true, it could do with a tidy,
And there's much grander places to be.
But our house, it's lived in and loved in,
And that makes it a palace to me.

The Things They Won't Remember

There are things they won't remember,
That you will never forget.
Their first birthday and Christmas,
Or the moment that you met.
There are times they won't remember,
They'll be some of the hardest of yours.
Endless weeks of colds and bugs,
Or sleepless nights spent pacing floors.
They will look back on your photos and ask,
"Did we really do all this stuff?"
They'll smile and they'll laugh
As you retell those days,
And you'll know you did more than enough.
Though they might not remember each second,
Not replay them the way that you do,
They'll remember that feeling
Of limitless love,
And remember it all came from you.

With Wonder

All each of us wants
Is to be happy.
To find glimmers
That light up our days.
And we all have our own little lights
That ignite our joy in some way.
But my child, they are endlessly happy.
There is nothing they need to find light.
They emit it with all of their being,
And their joy shines so beautifully bright.
Their love for this world is so pure,
And their glimmers are more like a flame.
Every day when I look at them smile,
I find myself doing the same.
When the leaves rustle, they listen.
And when the breeze blows on their skin,
They pause to feel all sensations
With wonder.
They stop and they take it all in.
And whenever I pause
And I watch them,
I feel myself bathe in their glow.
They live in each moment,
For all that it offers –
They're the happiest person I know.

Let There Be Mess!

Let there be mess!
Where one day there won't.
Let them talk endlessly,
Because one day they don't.
One day you might find
They don't have much to say.
That they'd rather stare
At a phone screen all day.
Let there be laughter,
Chaos, and noise.
Let there be teddies,
Books, and toys.
One day you might find
That your home is quite bare,
So neat and so tidy
With nobody there.
So let there be day trips,
Adventures, late nights.
Let there be silliness,
Games, water fights.
Let there be memories,
And let them be good.
Let them be little
And enjoy childhood.

So Lucky, So Perfect

Do you ever stop and look at your child
Doing something so simple,
Just sitting by your side,
And stare in wonder
At the little profile of their face,
Their nose, eyelashes, little chin?
You look down at their hands,
So perfect, their skin,
Your eyes full of tears,
A lump in your throat,
And you think,
"I am so lucky,
You are so perfect,
How is it possible you're mine?"

A Friend for Life

How wonderful to watch your little people
Become best friends.
To love each other,
Care for each other,
Look out for each other.
To watch them collapse in fits of laughter
At something so daft.
Or to comfort one another if they're sad,
To pick each other up if they need to.
To look at them curled up on the sofa watching the telly,
And feel so glad that they'll always have each other.

Buttery Toast

My Dad is seventy-five
And he tells me often
How his mum would walk to the school gates at break,
And bring him buttery toast.
He was five but he still cherishes that memory of his mum.
It's not the big stuff your children will remember
    most about you,
Not fancy days out,
Or expensive gifts.
It's all the little things:
The way you brush their hair.
The way your read their favourite book,
    the silly voices you put on.
The song you sing if they can't sleep.
The way you scoop them up if they fall.
Holding their hands,
Making their favourite breakfast,
The soup you make if they're poorly.
Running around the garden laughing,
Letting them sneak into your bed for a cuddle.
It's the buttery toast.
Don't worry so much about the big things.
The little ones, they matter the most.

Sunshine

You are sunshine.
You're a wonder.
You are magic.
But you're real.
And ever since I met you
That's exactly how I feel.

That my days are full of magic –
I'm so lucky, I can't say.
And even under rain clouds,
You bring sunshine every day.

Let's Play for a Minute

I'm just going to clear up the dishes.
I'll just put this washing away.
Sometimes it seems like I say, "Just a minute!"
One million times in a day.
Today the sun is shining,
Tomorrow, who knows, it might rain.
You won't ever be so little,
And we'll never get this day again.
So today let the dishes pile up –
The washing can wait one more day.
I'm taking a break
From "Just a minute".
Today, let's just make time to play.

Goodnight, Little One

I checked in on you,
Like I do every night.
Pushed your hair from your face
In the dim, soft light.
Somehow it seemed,
Though it couldn't be so,
That you'd grown since I left
Just an hour ago.
All of a sudden
You've gotten so tall,
You fill up that bed
That once made you so small.
I lean down and kiss you
And whisper goodnight,
Then I pause as I leave
To take in that sweet sight.
It's hard to believe
That it won't always be,
You safe in your bed
At home here with me.

Our 'Do You Remember?' Days

I know that right now
We're living through
Some of *the* days.
The ones we'll talk about
When we're old and grey.
They are our
'Do you remember?' days,
The ones we'll reminisce about.
We wake up together on Sunday mornings,
Little feet walking softly across the landing,
Climbing into bed between us.
We spend so much time together,
Doing simple things,
Having the best time.
Making memories.
These days aren't always easy.
They are almost always exhausting
In one way or another.
But we are so surrounded by our love for each other.
These are some of the best days of our lives.

Take Our Photo

Take our photo.
Not just partners but friends, relatives.

Just take our photo
When we don't ask for it,
When we aren't ready.
Even if we protest sometimes.

Take our photo
whilst we're feeding, running, playing,
Holding our children close.
When we've fallen asleep on the sofa with them,
Walking along holding hands.

Take our photo
When we're doing all the little things
   that make us their mum.
These are the photos that we'll frame,
That we'll treasure.
The ones that we'll cling to and say,
"Oh, I wish I could go back".

Take our photo.
I don't want perfectly posed photos and videos
Of Christmases or birthdays.
I want the photos of the imperfect, messy everyday life.
So I can look back and remember
How wonderful it all was.

Sitting Here With You

To some it might seem boring,
A rather mundane thing to do.
But if you asked me of perfection,
I'd say it's sitting here with you.

Sunday Mornings

Sleepy little feet
Padding down the hall
On Sunday mornings
Is the sweetest sound of all.

Slow Down, Kid

Each Day I Love You More

If we had forever together,
It still wouldn't be enough.
Watching you grow up is such an honour,
And yet so tough.
You are constantly changing –
Somehow each day I love you more.
I adore each version of you,
And miss the one that came before.

I'll Always See

If I'm ever walking without them
(Which isn't very often, but it does happen)
And I see something I know they'd like –
It could be something so simple,
Like a squirrel, or a tractor,
Or a duck, or a cute dog,
Or a weird looking tree,
Or a character they like on the side of a bus –
My heart jumps a little.
And I want to look down and say,
"Hey! Look at that!"
I know how their little face would light up,
And I smile anyway, even though they aren't there.
I can almost hear them laughing and chatting.
Maybe I'll tell them when I pick them up from school,
Or when I get home.
But mostly I forget.
I think that's how it will always be.
They'll get older,
They'll walk beside me a little less.
But in my heart I will always see the cute dogs,
The tractors, the ducks, the rainbows,
The really good puddles for jumping in,
The trees, the birds, the pebbles.
I'll always see it all,
Because they showed it to me.

And it can't be unseen.
And when they do walk beside me
(so much taller now)
We'll see it together still, and I'll smile.
Because I will always be a mum
To that little kid, always.
Even when they aren't so little anymore.

Let Me Keep Them

I have trouble parting
With those little sleep suits.
I've got bags full up with cardis, tiny vests,
And woolly boots.
I don't know why I keep them –
I know they're of no use.
I just can't help but cling to them.
I've really no excuse.

I know that you've outgrown them,
And they're never going to fit,
But sometimes, if I'm honest,
I just like to go and sit,
Unpack them, smell them, hold them,
Dream of when they did.
To think how you were so tiny,
It's hard to believe it.

One day, I'm sure before too long,
I'll manage to let go.
It's just I'm scared that when I do, it's you that will follow.
And before my eyes,
It's your childhood you'll outgrow.
So though it might seem silly,
They comfort me and so
I'll keep my woolly boots, and baby grows.

You Can

People are going to underestimate you through your life.
I will never be one of them.

People will say you won't achieve things.
I'll tell them that you will.

People will tell you all the things that you can't do.
I will point out all of those that you can.

People will try to hurry you along,
Try to rush you,
I will tell you to take your time.

People will think that you don't understand,
But I know that you do.

I will always be by your side,
I will always find words when you can't,
And I will never give up on you.

You are brilliant
And wonderful
In your own way.
And we will show the world that together.

Slow Down, Kid

Slow down, kid.
Don't grow so fast.
I want these few short years to last.
When I can hold you in my arms
And simple things still hold their charms.
When everything I show you is new
And all of it is fun to you.
When it's easy to make you smile.
I know this will only last a while.
When you still think I'm the whole world,
And in my arms you can lay curled.
Somehow these days go fast and slow,
But I can't bear to let them go.
Slow down, kid.
Let's not wish them away.
I'm happy here in these sweet days.

Sundays

I hope they come home on Sundays
With their washing,
Or hangovers.
With their news of the week that they had.
Maybe one day
with their own family.
I hope they walk through the door
Like it's their own
(Of course it always will be),
Throw their arms around my neck,
Sink into the sofa
And know that they're home.

How Far Will You Go?

I wonder how far you will go from me.
Will you travel the world,
Will you cross the blue sea?
Will you find a new home, and where will that be?
Wherever you are, I hope you feel free.

I wonder how far those feet will go.
Will they always go fast,
Or learn to go slow?
I wonder how your face will change
As you grow,
And about the new you
Who I've yet to know.

I wonder how high those feet will climb,
And cherish this time that they walk beside mine.
I hope that you'll give me a call
time to time,
To let your old mum know you're doing just fine.

First Days

I get a tear in my eye
When I think of little feet
Walking into a big busy hall, trying to find a seat.
Next to someone kind,
Another friendly little face,
My heart aches when I think of you taking your place.
As you sit down to your dinner,
Your legs swinging as you eat,
I wonder what you talk about
   with everyone you meet.
And when I think of playtime,
A lump settles in my throat.
Because I know sometimes you
    struggle with the zipper on your coat.
I hope that someone helps you,
Perhaps a teacher passing by,
And I hope that someone comforts you
   if you should fall and cry.
I don't always find it easy
To picture you without me,
But I know you're in good hands
And it's the best place for you to be.

My Daughter

My daughter is strong,
Her voice is heard.
Her feelings matter.
She can wear what she wants,
She can say what she wants,
She can be whoever
She wants to be.

My Shadow

Me and my shadow,
My shadow and me.
Wherever I'd go,
There my shadow would be.

Sometimes I'd say, "Shoo!
Get from under my feet".
Then I'd turn back around
And my shadow I'd meet.

My little shadow,
My shadow and me.
We were peas in a pod,
Just as close as could be.

But then one day,
When the sun did shine,
I looked for that shadow
And I found only mine.

My shadow was off in the world –
How's that so?
That my little shadow could suddenly grow.

They outgrew my shadow,
And off they went.
But that didn't mean our days were spent.

Now two long shadows,
We walk in the sun.
Still so many days
For us to have fun.

My lovely shadow,
My shadow and me,
Still peas in a pod
And as close as can be.

This Coat Belongs to Someone

This coat belongs to someone
Who means the world to me.
And they are only little,
So please treat them carefully.

This bag belongs to someone
Who's having a first day.
So if you see them looking lost,
Please help them on their way.

This jumper belongs to someone
Who might be missing Mum.
They could use a friend or two,
I hope that they find some.

Those shoes belong to someone
Who usually walks beside me.
Who I'll be thinking of the whole day long
And I can't wait to see.

Proud of everything you are,
And proud of all that you'll become.
Proud of everything you do,
And proud to call myself your mum.

More People Who Care About People

Sometimes I worry
That I'm raising
A sensitive person,
In this insensitive world.
But then I remember
That what the world needs
Is more people
Who see kindness
As strength,
And never as weakness.
And more people
Who care
About people.

Tea

One evening I'll sit down,
There will be no bath to run,
And no books to read.

No little voices in the hall,
No laughter bouncing off the walls,
No chaos here – just me.

I'll look around at the empty room,
I'll sigh (I'll probably cry).
I'll reach for my phone, send you a text,
Then go make myself some tea.

My Boy

My boy,
I see you
And everything you are,
And it's far more than anything
That I could ever hope to be.

My boy,
I love you,
For everything you are.
You're just so endlessly
And effortlessly better than me.

My boy,
I know you,
And everything you are,
And I'm proud of every part of you,
And you should be proud too.

My boy,
I adore you,
And everything you are.
I know that you'll spread joy in this world
Whatever you go on and do.

The Line

Every day for such a long time
You've stood there in that line,
With mums and dads
And familiar faces.
At first it felt weird
But it's one of those places
That starts off scary when its new
But so soon becomes a part of you.
Cemented in your daily routine:
"Have you got your books?
Are your teeth clean?"
Then you're out of the door,
And it's to that front gate.
More often than not, you're a little bit late.
You give them a kiss,
And they're off on their way,
And you tell them you'll see them at the end of the day.
You wave to their teacher –
Oh, they're just lovely.
They're everything you hoped a teacher would be.
They're kind and they listen,
And you know that they care.
So they make this whole business more easy to bear.

It was only a school,
And it was never forever,
But each day in the line you've stood there together
and you've braved the lovely English weather.
"Nip under this brolly, you'll get soaking wet!"
Sending notes to the WhatsApp
So no one forgets
That it's sports day next week.
"Can you make it, or no?
I'll cheer yours on too if I'm able to go."
And you've gone through a childhood
And all that it brings.
You've stood in the hall,
And you've watched them all sing
With a lump in your throat,
And tears in your eyes.
And you've marvelled together
How quick the time flies.
And before you know it
You're saying goodbye.
There's a first and a last day,
And you'd never have guessed
That the last is the worst
And the first was the best.
Now they're off on the bus,
Or they're walking with friends,
And you're holding your breath

Until that day ends.
And you're missing that line,
And that hug at the gate.
One more frantic morning of shouting, "We're late!"
New parents, new faces, move into that line.
And you'll miss it, you both will,
But you're going to be fine.
You got through it together,
You both learnt and you grew,
And whatever comes next,
That'll be okay too.

I Will Make Your Voice Be Heard

Oh what I'd give to sit beside you,
And hear you talk about your day.
Or overhear you saying something sweet
And funny as you play.
I'd love to hear you chatter,
Or hear your voice call out my name.
People say it doesn't matter,
But I'd love to all the same.
I wonder what's your favourite colour –
Do you have one? I do too.
I wonder what you're really thinking
When I sit and chat to you.
I wonder if you know the alphabet,
Or how to count to ten.
I wonder, years from now,
Will things be any different then?
I would never hope to change you,
You're perfect to me,
But it kills me that whatever's on your mind
Can't be set free.
I hope that as you grow
I hear the things that go unsaid.
And if I only had one wish,
Then I would see inside your head.

But if it's always this way,
If you don't ever say a word,
I will say them for you.
I will make your voice be heard.

One Day

One day, you and I
Will stand shoulder to shoulder.
Your eyes will sparkle just the same,
   I'm sure,
Though your face has grown older.
And I'll have aged too, of course,
My hair a lot more grey.
But I'll always be your mum,
And love you the same way.
Gone will be those days
Of baths, books, and bed.
You'll be asking me for lifts,
Or a tenner instead.
And there will come a day
When you walk out of our door,
And I guess that this won't be your house anymore.
But if I'm still here,
Or wherever I'll be,
Then you'll find your home
Because your home is me.

Dream Girl

I dreamt of little tea sets,
And afternoons spent sipping air.
I dreamt of princess dresses,
And of ribbons in your hair.

I dreamt of painting pictures,
Little love notes, wobbly words.
I dreamt of little verses,
Sung so sweetly, my song bird.

I dreamt we'd hold hands walking
Through tall flowers, you and me.
But I never dreamt up half the things
That you'd turn out to be.

Standing in a tutu, welly boots,
With arms crossed tight.
Such a tiny little person,
Putting up the greatest fight.

I didn't dream you'd stamp your feet at me,
Your fists bunched at your side.
Or how much I could feel your pain,
Each time you fell and cried.

Or how it would destroy me,
If someone ever made you sad.
I didn't dream that someone else's pain
Could ever feel so bad.

I dreamt I'd have a daughter,
I didn't know it would be you.
But in everything you've come to be
You've made my dreams come true.

And there are endless flowers,
But we don't walk, we run.
Together hand in hand,
Long shadows in the sun.

I could never have dreamt
That you would love me like you do.
I dreamt I'd have a daughter,
And I'm so glad she is you.

There Will Always Be a Place Here With Me

There will always be a place for you at my table.
There will always be an ear
If you ever need a chat.
I can't promise that I'll always have the answers,
But I promise that I'll listen,
I can promise you that.
There will always be a chair for you to sit on,
A place for you to sleep,
Should you ever need a bed.
There will always be somewhere for you to go to
If you just need to sit in silence,
Or to clear your busy head.
There will always be a space for you at my house.
No matter your age,
And no matter mine.
If you ever need support,
If you've made mistakes,
Or you feel lost.
You will always and forever
Find my arms open wide.

The Sunflowers

My eldest boy goes walking
In amongst the sunflowers.
Never did I dream
That he'd get quite so tall.
I thought these days
Would last so much longer,
But the truth is they passed by
In no time at all.

Their Light

Another World

I think there must be another world,
And it's one where you and I
Are sitting side by side
With our arms
Around one another,
And we're staring at the sky.
And we wonder
How on earth could it ever be
That somewhere there's a world
With no you, and just a me.
Because you and I are one,
But we've been split in two.
It seems impossible that there's a me
Without a you.
But there isn't, not really –
I carry you with me.
In my heart and my soul
Is where you'll always be.
And I watch from this world
For all your little signs.
They'll pull me through these days,
Until that time arrives
When we're together again,
Sitting side by side,
With our arms around one another,
Gazing at the sky.

Their Light

Their light will never leave our lives,
Or this world.
They will always be a part of us,
A part of our story.
For every single day,
For the rest of our lives,
They will always be with us.

I Know You

I didn't know you,
That's what people think.
I didn't hear your voice,
I didn't hear you sing.
I didn't see you twirl
In a princess dress.
I didn't pack up a hospital bag,
Little vests.
I didn't know you,
I've never seen your face,
Just an outline, a blur,
In that clinical place.
I didn't know you
When they said that you'd gone.
People mutter, "Oh well,
Keep trying, move on."
As if I didn't know you
In a million different ways,
As if I hadn't pictured
The rest of our days.
With you, my baby,
Who was life within me.
How strange and insensitive
This world can be.

I knew you, I know you,
I dream of you still.
I knew you, I know you,
And I always will.

Two little feet

Two little feet
That never took a step.
But you carry them with you
Wherever you go.
Two little footprints
Etched on your heart – forever.
Wherever yours are,
Theirs follow.
But how you wish they could feel
The sand between their toes.
Or the grass in the summer,
Or the breeze when it blows.
But you feel them in it all,
Beside you – always.

Butterfly

Where are you going to, butterfly?
Won't you stay here with me?
There's so many things I imagined we'd do,
But I guess they were not meant to be.
Where are you going to, butterfly?
People will say, "Now they're free."
When I look for you
In the big open blue,
It's a butterfly that I will see.

A Mother's Love

A mother's love protects,
It builds a shield around you
That will stay with you forever.
It's so strong,
And so pure,
That even when she's gone,
Her love shines on.
Like a beautiful aura,
You might not see it,
But it surrounds you
Always.
And will do
For all of your days.

ACKNOWLEDGEMENTS

I would like to thank a few people for their help with *All of My Days*.

Firstly, to Hazel at Fox & Ink Books, who gave me the opportunity to finally bring this book to life after years of hoping for it to be. Secondly, to all the team at Fox & Ink, who are so supportive and passionate about what they do. Their pride for publishing is contagious, and I am so pleased to be working with them again. I would also like to say a huge thank you to my editor Jasmine – without her, there wouldn't be any full stops anywhere at all in these pages! She has been such a help, and I really appreciate her encouragement. Her belief in these words has really given me the confidence to share them with you all.

I would love to thank every single person who supports me on my Instagram page, and all of the mums who relate to and share my poems and drawings. Without you all, this book would never have become a reality, and I can't thank you enough.

My husband Jordan, who has a front-row seat for all these outpourings of emotions – thank you for always being my calm in the chaos.

Lastly, I have to thank my three children. You have brought so much wonder to my life. Without you three, I don't think I would see even half as much beauty in this world. Thank you for showing it to me. You have my whole heart, forever.

ABOUT THE AUTHOR

KERRI CUNNINGHAM, aka Murphy's sketches, is a writer and artist from Preston in Lancashire. She lives in a small village with her husband and three children.

She has always loved drawing and writing and went to study Fine Art many years ago at the University of Lancashire. In recent years, she has used her sketches and writing to bring some joy to people's day via her social media platform – Murphy's Sketches. She works full time as an artist and writer selling cards and prints.

She loves to spend time outside with her family, and shared her love of the outdoors and making the most of all the little things throughout the year in her first children's book, *There is a Season*.

Kerri's debut picture book, *Baxter's View*, celebrates neurodiversity and encourages people to slow down and look at the world in a different way.

Find out more by visiting:

www.instagram.com\murphys_sketches

murphyssketches.co.uk

www.foxandinkbooks.com